Ocean Friends

HARP SEALS

Aven King

PowerKiDS
press™

New York

Published in 2016 by The Rosen Publishing Group, Inc.
29 East 21st Street, New York, NY 10010

First Edition

Editor: Caitie McAneney
Book Design: Katelyn Heinle

Photo Credits: Cover, pp. 1, 10 Jennifer Hayes/National Geographic/Getty Images; cover (series logo coral vector design) Koryaba/Shutterstock.com; back cover mycteria/Shutterstock.com; pp. 3–24 (interior coral vector design) etraveler/Shutterstock.com; p. 5 AleksandrN/Shutterstock.com; pp. 6, 24 (flipper) CORDIER Sylvain/hemis.fr/Getty Images; p. 9 Purestock/Thinkstock.com; p. 13 Vladimir Melnik/Shutterstock.com; p. 14 Tom Brakefield/Thinkstock.com; pp. 17, 24 (pup) FloridaStock/Shutterstock.com; p. 18 Bill Curtsinger/National Geographic/Getty Images; p. 21 MudmanDave/Thinkstock.com; p. 22 Brian J. Skerry/National Geographic/Getty Images.

Library of Congress Cataloging-in-Publication Data

King, Aven, author.
 Harp seals / Aven King.
     pages cm. — (Ocean friends)
 Includes index.
 ISBN 978-1-5081-4172-3 (pbk.)
 ISBN 978-1-5081-4173-0 (6 pack)
 ISBN 978-1-5081-4174-7 (library binding)
 1. Harp seal—Juvenile literature. 2. Seals (Animals)—Juvenile literature. I. Title.
 QL737.P64K56 2016
 599.79'29—dc23
                                        2015023506

Manufactured in the United States of America

CPSIA Compliance Information: Batch #BW16PK: For Further Information contact Rosen Publishing, New York, New York at 1-800-237-9932

CONTENTS

Harp seals live in cold ocean waters.

flippers

Harp seals have **flippers**.
Flippers help them swim.

Harp seals have fat called blubber to keep them warm.

Harp seals close their eyes, ears, and nose when they swim.

Mother seals have their babies on ice in the ocean. A baby harp seal is called a **pup**.

A mother harp seal can tell her baby apart from other babies by its smell.

Baby harp seals have white fur.
The fur is very soft.

Baby harp seals lose their white fur as they grow.

Adult harp seals shed their coat every year. Their coat is spotted.

Harp seals dive deep into the water for fish. They're great swimmers!

WORDS TO KNOW

flipper

pup

INDEX

WEBSITES

Due to the changing nature of Internet links, PowerKids Press has developed an online list of websites related to the subject of this book. This site is updated regularly. Please use this link to access the list: www.powerkidslinks.com/ocea/harp